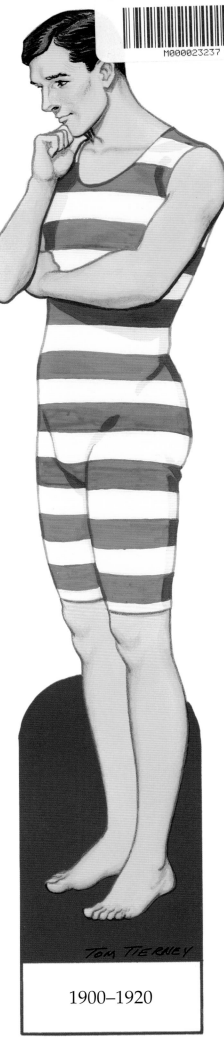

1900–1920

1900–1920

Plate 1

Do not cut out
spaces between
arms and body.

1900–1920

1900–1920

Plate 2

'20s

1920s

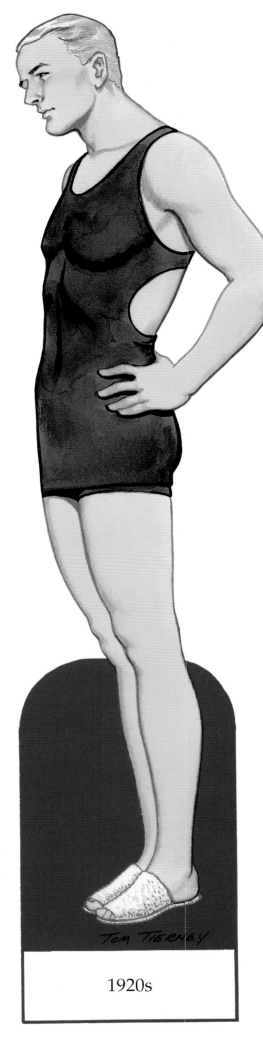

1920s

Plate 3

Do not cut out
spaces between
arms and body.

1920s

1920s

Plate 4

1930s

1930s

Plate 5

1930s   1930s

Plate 6

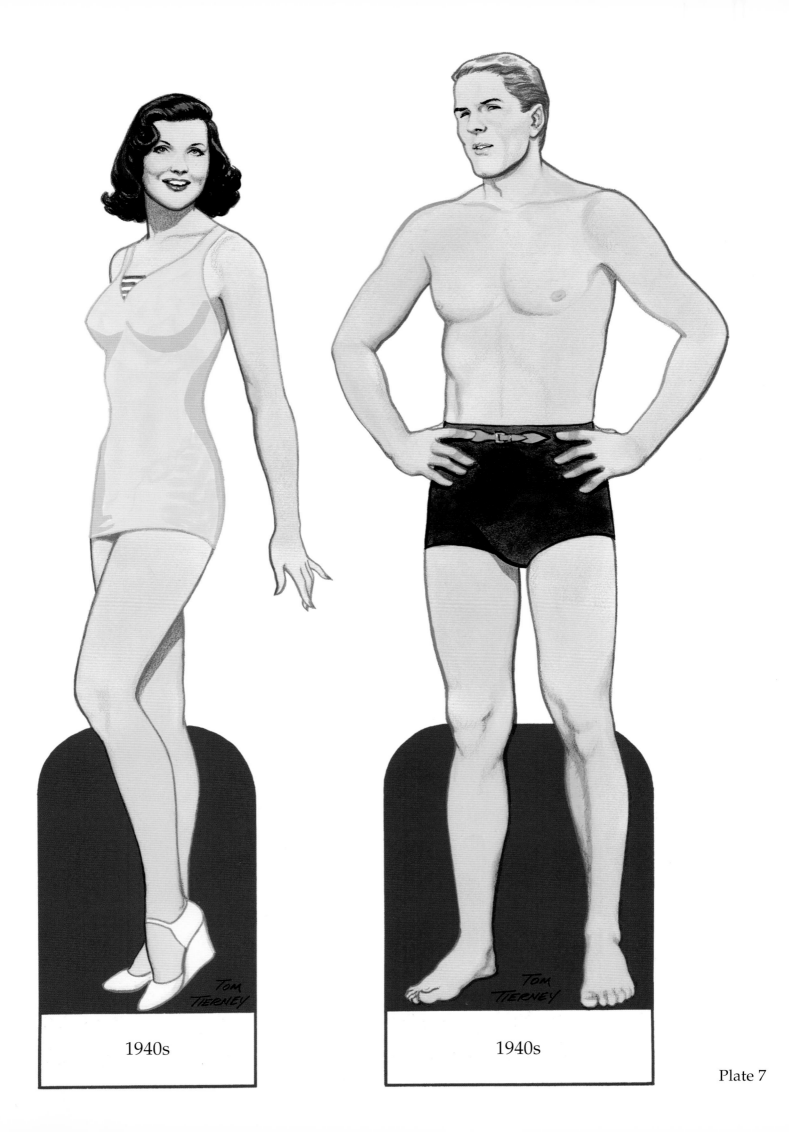

1940s

1940s

Plate 7

1940s

1940s

Plate 8

1950s

1950s

Plate 9

Do not cut out
spaces between
arms and bodies.

1950s

1950s

Plate 10

1960s

1960s

Plate 11

Plate 12   1960s   1960s

1970s

1970s

Plate 13

Do not cut out space between arm and body.

1970s

1970s

Plate 14

1980s

1980s

Plate 15

1980s

1980s

Plate 16